For Your Garden

GARDEN SHEDS AND POTTING AREAS

For Your Garden

GARDEN SHEDS AND POTTING AREAS

PENELOPE O'SULLIVAN

FRIEDMAN/FAIRFAX
PUBLISHERS

A FRIEDMAN/FAIRFAX BOOK

© 1998 by Michael Friedman Publishing Group, Inc.

Library of Congress Cataloging-in-Publication Data available upon request

ISBN 1-56799-698-1

Editor: Susan Lauzau
Art Director: Jeff Batzli
Designer: Jennifer Markson
Photography Editor: Sarah Storey
Production Manager: Ingrid Neimanis-McNamara

Color separations by Fine Arts Repro House Co., Ltd.
Printed in Hong Kong by Midas Printing, Ltd.

3 5 7 9 10 8 6 4

For bulk purchases and special sales, please contact:
Friedman/Fairfax Publishers
Attention: Sales Department
15 West 26th Street
New York, NY 10010
212/685-6610 FAX 212/685-1307

Visit our website:
http://www.metrobooks.com

Table of Contents

INTRODUCTION

Garden sheds have many uses, both practical and decorative. In these basic, boxy structures, form follows function. A roof and four walls protect gardening equipment and shelter us as we accomplish gardening tasks. Here, we gardeners may store our tools, plant seeds, prick out seedlings, pot up plants and bulbs, condition cut blooms, and dry flowers and herbs. Sometimes a shed is simply a good place to think. We can sit on a cast-off chair and jot notes in our garden journal or thumb through plant and seed catalogues for inspiration.

Sheds, however, are no Johnny-come-lately to the garden. They've been present in many forms for generations. Potting sheds were commonplace on nineteenth-century country estates, where they were situated near the kitchen garden's tidy rows of vegetables, herbs, and cutting flowers for the house. The shed was a sensible place, containing materials necessary for the efficient production of food for the household. Seeds, pots, catalogues, rubber boots, a workbench, and bins of potting soil filled much of the space. Sometimes, especially on smaller properties, potting sheds were part of other garden buildings like greenhouses or toolsheds.

For more than a century, multipurpose garden sheds have been a familiar presence in our backyards. We often think of them as essential but uninspiring buildings stuck on the lawn. Yet these structures, built of brick, wood, or stone, don't have to look dull. With simple landscaping techniques and the careful selection of plants and building materials, sheds can become an integral part of the landscape, lending charm and stability to our garden designs. The act of walking down a garden path, too, is as old and revered as gardening itself. Sometimes it is merely the infinitely practical act of moving from one part of the garden to another. At others times, the movements are simply the back and forth of a busy gardener as he or she tends to the beds along the path. There are yet other moments when nothing is more romantic than a stroll along a woodland path with the one you love.

ABOVE: Garden sheds lend themselves to the creative reuse of building materials. The rural character of this unassuming toolshed derives from wooden boards that were recycled from an old grain silo. Because it is used only for storage, a small window cut into the shed provides all the lighting needed.

OPPOSITE: This quaint garden cottage shows the influence of the arts-and-crafts movement and English vernacular architecture in its half-timbered walls, red slate roof, and little gabled entry. Adding to the cottage's storybook charm are red roses, deep burgundy clematis, and the bright purple flower spikes of delphiniums.

ABOVE: Effective landscaping helps tailor the site to accommodate a large garden building. Bordering the path to the shed, mugo pine, veronica, sedum, *Nepeta* × *faassenii* 'Six Hill's Giant', and *Betula platyphylla* var. *japonica* 'Whitespire' weave a tapestry of purple, yellow, and green.

ABOVE: Tulips and daffodils bring bright spring color to the landscape surrounding a large, unadorned garden shed. This gardener has elected to let the flowers, rather than the building, carry the garden show, and keeps the focus on the plants by leaving the shed's plain wooden boards to weather naturally.

ABOVE: This lavishly bordered path leads to a vine-covered garden shed. A profusion of blooms and greenery nearly obscures the shed, which is used mainly to start seeds in early spring. Dense, low, perennial hedges structure the border, which includes white roses, foxgloves, and a strawberry jar filled with succulents.

RIGHT: Attached to a glasshouse, this garden shed has an inviting air of mystery. Ancient vines climb heavily on the front wall, arching over the door and crumbling the stucco in their path. A cluster of pinks sweetens the air with the fragrance of spicy cloves. Bamboo stakes, a sign of active gardening, lean against the glasshouse, ready to bring order to lax stems.

ABOVE: A trio of potted Transvaal daisies (*Gerbera jamesonii*) sit on a shelf outside a potting shed window, while cosmos and holly-hocks grow nearby. Transvaal daisies are popular greenhouse plants, which are perennial in the hot climate of their native South Africa. Any favorite potted flower will look stunning given such a treatment—the effect is similar to that of a windowbox, but it is easier to change the display with these highly portable pots.

OPPOSITE: In order to better fit the design of this lattice green-house and potting shed into the surrounding garden, the sheared shrubbery beyond the building echoes its curving roof. Moreover, the stone wall, the hedges, and the rose beds run parallel to the side of the shed, reinforcing the neat geometry of the garden.

ABOVE LEFT: A vine-covered pergola, raised beds, a brick red garden shed, and containers filled with flowers are key features of this orderly garden. The ogee arch, created by the double S-curves of the pergola, adds a Moorish touch to the hardscape. The repetition of the arches creates a visual tunnel that carries the gaze straight back towards the house, while the pale gravel paths make a striking visual and textural contrast with the dark wood of the pergola and shed.

ABOVE: A few plants and props can transform an ordinary garden setting into a truly magical one. Here, forget-me-nots (*Myosotis* spp.), a magnificent 'Climbing Coral Sunset' rose, a large clay urn, and a couple of antique wheels create a romantic scene outside a weathered wooden shed.

LEFT: Trellises make the difference for this delightful potting shed, transforming it from a boxy white building into a country cottage smothered in roses and clematis. Rainbow-colored blooms of various heights and shapes adorn the surrounding flower beds. This homey hodgepodge is the very essence of cottage-garden appeal.

LEFT: Whimsical paint colors dress up this wooden garden shed. Its bright yellow door creates a focal point at the end of the path, while dusty blue adorns the trim on the pitched roof. A pillar tinted lavender-blue supports a 'Dortmund' rose, a winter-hardy, disease-free climber that sports fragrant, five-petaled, crimson flowers with white centers. 'Dortmund' blooms profusely in midseason and offers good repeat; big red rosehips add interest through autumn. Red, blue, and yellow—the primary colors—transform this corner of the garden into a visual treat, as well as a place in which to take care of essential gardening tasks.

OPPOSITE: A roomy shed with the quiet character of a barn opens onto a garden notable for its simplicity. Situated at the far end of the garden, the shed offers a stopping point for the eye, defining the area where cultivation ends and the wild woods begin. Daylilies (*Hemerocallis* spp.) and lilies (*Lilium* spp.) border the lawn, which is enclosed by walls of stacked granite boulders. The pastoral tableau created by the sundial, the wooden wheelbarrow, and the shepherd's crook adds to the peaceful ambience of the scene.

ABOVE: A long compost fork affixed to a batten door proclaims the shed's intended use and provides accent for an otherwise commonplace structure. The unpainted cedar shakes covering the building link it to its natural surroundings, creating a pleasing rustic look. Near the door, a bird's nest spruce grows in a mulched bed in front of the climbing hybrid tea rose, 'Aloha'.

ABOVE: A cluster of purple clematis blossoms and neatly pruned mounds of *Buxus sempervirens* complement this toolshed's shake roof with its scalloped decoration. The attached root cellar, which can be accessed by a set of double doors set at a 45-degree angle, is useful for storing produce from the garden as well as for overwintering tender bulbs.

Chapter One

THE GARDEN BUILDING AS LANDSCAPE ORNAMENT

The garden shed can be more than a utilitarian presence in the garden. Its outer doors and walls create a backdrop for a picture of country life. Sometimes that picture is quite literal—for example, a two-dimensional mural of a rural garden painted on a suburban storage shed or a garage help spin a bucolic fantasy.

Sometimes the look is three-dimensional, composed of artfully arranged implements propped against a weathered wall. Pitchforks, spades, scythes, rakes, and other garden tools symbolize the pastoral life—that harmonious interplay of man and nature we yearn to achieve. These tableaux, landscaped with shrubs and flowers, can capture the spirit of country life in just a corner of the garden. The best images posess the power of icons, familiar but transcendent. They nod at our need to connect with that ultimately untamable tigress, Mother Nature, and can bring either humor or gravity to a cultivated place.

Often, the walls of a shed extend the garden, creating, by the simple addition of trellises, support for vines and other climbers. Along with shrubs, hedges, and tall flower borders, vines can mask a plain building or lend character to a handsome one. Roses, clematis, and wisteria bring romance to a bare wall. Honeysuckle and morning glories vie for homey appeal, while passionflower, canary bird vine, and Dutchman's pipe are equally desirable but more unusual.

Yet a well-styled garden building can also stand alone, relying more on its setting in the landscape than on its paint colors or floral disguise. Sheds like these add magic to the landscape, bringing a human scale to grand vistas and engendering an appreciation of the smallest details.

ABOVE: This small garden shed features a tall rectangular window that admits extra light. When the door is open, the interior of the shed is entirely lit, making it easy to locate tools, bags of potting soil, garden gloves, and other accessories. Fragrant and beautiful, the roses that line the path delight the senses of sight and smell.

OPPOSITE: Ficus, Japanese maple (*Acer palmatum*), crape-myrtle (*Lagerstroemia indica*), and a vine-smothered storage shed form the bones of this lightly shaded garden. The overgrown quality of the corner lends an air of mystery and age to the building, fostering the impression that it has existed from time immemorial.

ABOVE: This gardener has doubled the impact of the flower border by replacing the window of the shed with a mirror. An easy and inexpensive improvement, the mirror not only "increases" the beauty of garden scenes, it hides the sometimes unsightly contents of the garden shed. In early summer, the mirrored window reflects a picture of foxgloves (*Digitalis* hybrids) and sweet William (*Dianthus barbatus*).

RIGHT: This large multipurpose shed is perfect for drying flowers and herbs–Dutch doors and windows that open at the top allow plenty of air circulation, which is critical when drying plants.

ABOVE LEFT: A quaint garden building, reminiscent of a child's play house, provides a shady and comfortable retreat from the heat of the day. A pot of annual vinca hangs near the entrance, and hostas and impatiens line the front wall.

ABOVE RIGHT: A coat of dark red paint, crisp white trim, and an old-fashioned batten door give this New England shed a rustic presence. A vine-covered arch paired with perennial daisies and purple coneflowers (*Echinacea purpurea*) form the backbone of the country garden surrounding the shed.

OPPOSITE: A window with white trim above a flower-filled window box turns this plain little shed, sited at the edge of a vegetable garden, into a charming garden feature. By painting the walls dark brown and screening the sides with tall hollyhocks and vines, the gardener draws our attention away from the shed to the abundance and beauty of nature.

LEFT: Instead of changing the appearance of this garden shed with plants or paint, the owners chose to let its wooden boards remain visible and turn naturally gray with age. Only select accents, such as window frames, sills, and hinges, have been given a hint of color. The rose pink flowers and strange, airy texture of the massed spider flower (*Cleome hasslerana*) contrasts boldly with the silver-hued shed and the dense richness of the nearby dwarf alberta spruce and other evergreens.

BELOW: Lavishly planted petunias and geraniums add polish to this country tableau at the side of a garden shed. These inexpensive annuals can provide brilliant color in the garden from late spring until frost. A well-placed garden fork, a spade, a wooden wagon wheel, and a window box are the other accessories that give this setting its down-home style. Properly situated in its lucky position, a horseshoe contributes its good wishes for the growing season.

ABOVE: An irregular stick fence and a rustic wood shed with a gambrel roof are tailored to the old-fashioned character of this garden. White spider flowers (*Cleome basslerana*) and nicotiana add to the garden's heirloom appeal.

ABOVE: This handsome garden shed fits in beautifully with its environment. The shed's wooden construction and the subtle earthy colors of its decoration complement its shady, wooded site. Rhododendrons and hostas humanize the scale of the landscape and show the gardener's hand in what might otherwise be a wild and untamed setting.

OPPOSITE: At the peak of autumn, maples carpet the ground with golden leaves near an old springhouse. Built into the hillside, this garden structure's design takes advantage of the natural terrain by becoming part of the living landscape instead of a prominent manmade intrusion. Property owners lucky enough to inherit vintage structures such as icehouses, chicken coops, springhouses, and so on often have enchanting, ready-made spaces for converting into garden storage or potting areas.

ABOVE: An arched entry can define the transition between formal and informal garden spaces. This arch frames a formal garden building and complements the garden's sophisticated design. Among the features of this varied garden are vine-covered arches, a classical urn, a fieldstone wall, plant-filled terra-cotta containers, and a border packed with irises, roses, and peonies.

OPPOSITE: Potted plants are an easy and decorative way to bring a splash of color to a shady spot in the garden. Here, petunias and impatiens in terra-cotta pots brighten the walls of a plain white potting shed, which is rimmed with ferns at its base. The containers have been easily and inexpensively attached to the walls by means of wire loops hung over nails.

ABOVE: A tiny shed provides all the storage needed for a small garden. Situated on the edge of a patio made of antique brick, the little garden house is complemented by well-placed containers filled with colorful flowers. Because most of the garden's color comes from potted annuals, the plants can change at little cost as the season progresses.

LEFT: This garden shed serves as an aviary, a place for keeping birds. As lovely living garden ornaments, birds can provide hours of backyard entertainment.

ABOVE: This colorful trompe l'oeil (French for "fool the eye") flower garden is a year-round reminder of country life. Painted on the side of a large shed, the mural has blooms ranging from red and pink tulips to purple pansies and violets. A vision of eternal spring, this trompe l'oeil appears to enlarge the actual growing space by extending the view along a painted garden path.

ABOVE: Set into a curving, red brick wall, this sturdy garden building with painted white trim lends an air of massive solidity to this Virginia garden. Mature plantings of shrubs and daylilies add to the look of permanence. Massed daylilies are an excellent choice for a prominent site. They provide a bold swath of color when in bloom and their straplike foliage looks excellent after the flowers have passed. Moreover, planting along the wall softens the appearance of the overall brick structure.

Chapter Two

OUTDOOR POTTING AREAS

Every gardener needs an area to work, a place to perform those myriad, behind-the-scenes tasks that make our gardens successful all season long. Yes, we can buy annuals already potted, but how much more creative and less expensive to make our own container gardens with pots and plants we choose and grow ourselves.

While some gardeners start seeds and pot up plants indoors, others prefer to do their chores outside. Gardeners with limited space may not even have a shed or an appropriate indoor space. Those of us with sheds may pack them full of tools and yard supplies, leaving no room to work inside.

Outdoor potting stations can be as varied as the imagination allows. They include old wooden benches, cupboards, or a corner of a lath house, where a gardener can find respite from the sun and heat. Sometimes a gardener will create a temporary potting area, setting up the necessary equipment near an outdoor dining table or on an empty patch of path or pavement. Potting soil, fertilizer, pots, seedlings, a pencil, and a pad of paper on which to sketch planting designs are useful items in the potting spot. It's a good idea to keep pictures from magazines and books on hand for inspiration, along with a plant dictionary to remind you of each plant's ultimate size and color.

ABOVE: Terra-cotta flowerpots planted with *Viola* 'Sorbet Yellow Frost' look especially attractive against the ruddy brick of this house. This plant thrives in the rich garden soil of cultivated beds and borders but also performs well under many other conditions, both in containers and in the ground. A tray with sturdy sides provides convenient transport for a small number of pots.

OPPOSITE: This attractive garden includes a small greenhouse and shelves for hardening off plants on their way into the garden. A countertop in the greenhouse provides space for potting up plants, while the table nearby can be pressed into service on the busiest gardening days. Plant-filled clay pots hang in an artistic arrangement on the high, mortared stone wall, which edges the garden and creates a private outdoor room for its owners.

ABOVE: Stacks of clay pots fill this verdant work area. Terra-cotta flowerpots, popular since the seventeenth century in Europe, look pleasing and, because of their porosity, promote good soil drainage. They must, however, be carefully cleaned to remove limescale and old dirt before reusing. Some of the cuttings in the foreground are in plastic pots, which retain moisture a bit longer than clay pots and therefore need less frequent watering.

OPPOSITE: A handsome potting table adds lived-in charm to this patio. The area consists of a large, waist-high trough of potting soil with a ledge for garden tools. A dried-flower arrangement on the brick wall, a piece of garden sculpture, and several ornamental potted plants tie the potting area into the combined decorative and utilitarian nature of the space.

OPPOSITE: A small-flowered clematis (*Clematis montana*) grows over a potting storage area at Kew Gardens. The shelves are tightly packed with tidy rows of clay pots in various sizes. While most home gardeners don't need this number of pots, a lesson in efficient but decorative storage can be learned from the masters.

RIGHT: This small but efficient potting area consists of open storage shelves above a larger work shelf. Large pieces of equipment like the soil screener, which do not fit on the shelves, lean against the wall below. A handsome wooden chest set below the window offers additional storage as well as a handy surface on which to set extra materials and reference books without subjecting them to the soil and wet of the potting table.

ABOVE: For convenience, it's hard to beat this potting cabinet with a lifting top. Set against the wall of the house, and tucked in beside a lattice screen, this simple cupboard accommodates empty pots, gloves, and soil amendments on its upper shelves and small tools, potting soil, and other neccessities in the cabinets below. Once raised, the structure's face becomes a roof, sheltering the gardener from the harsh rays of the sun.

LEFT: Flowering bulbs can be forced indoors in a heated potting shed, where they can be kept out of sight until they begin to bloom. Forced bulbs offer brilliant, relatively long-lasting blooms for the house during the winter, and can be planted to coincide with special events or holidays.

OPPOSITE: A yellow ladder-style case holding a brightly colored array of potted petunias serves as the focus of a simple outdoor potting area. Pots painted in stripes or in solid yellow and green add to the ladder's decorative effect. On the nearby pavement are more plants in containers, a watering can, and stacks of pots. The overall effect is jumbled but delightful, with the gardener's personality very much in evidence.

OPPOSITE: This structure, made of wooden posts, beams, fencing, and an arbor-like roof is an ideal spot for a potting area. Open to breezes yet protected from the sun, it has plenty of room for spreading out seed trays and potting up plants for the garden. A stunning vintage window complements the old-fashioned gingerbread trim and lends character to the building.

ABOVE: This attractive potting area holds all the necessities: a long worktable, a storage shelf for plants already potted, drawers to hold seeds, small tools, catalogues, pens, and paper, and storage bins for soil, compost, vermiculite, and other potting amendments. A wheelbarrow sits nearby, ready to carry the potted plants to their new homes in the garden and to collect plants past their prime for renewal or disposal. The use of lattice for the potting enclosure provides both protection from the wind and privacy by screening the potting area from the rest of the garden.

ABOVE: Potting up plants does not require an abundance of space. Even a shelf set at counter height can do the job admirably. Here, potted chrysanthemums, together with several accoutrements of potting, sit on a narrow shelf attached to a barn wall.

RIGHT: A resourceful gardener created this rabbit-proof potting area out of lattice and wire. Tender young plants can size up unmolested by wild creatures before being set out into the garden. For convenience and accessibility, a large, raised container, similar to a sandbox, holds potting soil. A mulched "floor" means never having to sweep up spilled soil.

Chapter Three

INDOOR POTTING AREAS

The potting shed is the nerve center of the garden, and the potting bench its soul. Here, the mystery of life begins anew. We fill flats or boxes with nourishing substance, the potting soil, sow seeds in rows or broadcast them on the loamy surface, add a fine layer of potting mix on top, and water the seeds in. Then the magic begins. Depending on conditions and germination times, seedlings appear in days or weeks and are soon ready to be pricked off and potted. Eventually they'll be ready for life in the garden, either potted or planted directly in the earth.

To complete our indoor chores, we'd like a sink or faucet in or near the shed, and a light source such as a window, a lamp, or an overhead bulb. Another necessity is storage space, including drawers, closed cupboards, and open shelves. These hold everything from string and boxes of labeling materials to seeds and bins of potting mix, compost, and fertilizers. Stacks of flowerpots in every size fill shelves, while a container of potsherds for drainage and a hammer to smash them stand nearby.

On hooks and nails pounded into the wall hang large and small tools like trowels, pitchforks, spades, shovels, and brooms. The most conscientious gardeners clean the dirt off their tools and rub them with oil to preserve them and banish rust. Equipment maintained this way lasts for years.

Garden records also belong in the shed. In these, we note the weather, spraying or fertilizing schedules when applicable, plant combinations that worked and those that didn't, and our observations on growing various trees, shrubs, flowers, and vegetables.

Although potting benches are usually high enough for a gardener to work standing up, a chair for pulling on boots or for taking a quick rest from gardening chores can be a useful addition to the room. With a portable heater in place, we can create herb or flower crafts with summer's dried harvest or thumb through the latest seed and plant catalogues when it's too cold to be outdoors.

OPPOSITE: Eclectic architectural details lend this potting room an abundance of traditional charm. Cornice moldings, a Dutch door, and decorative gables around the door frame and again above the potting bench give the structure a fanciful character. Lush plantings surrounding the doorway and on the steps add enchanting color and texture to the garden.

RIGHT: Many vegetables can be started indoors six to eight weeks before the last frost, to ensure the earliest possible harvest. Delicate seedlings can be grown indoors and then gradually acclimated to the cooler weather outside. This crop of lettuce and salad greens waits in a sunny spot on the potting table to be moved out into the garden.

ABOVE: The size of a glasshouse determines the number and the layout of shelves or benches. Most benches have a depth of two to three feet, which makes it easy to reach from front to back when caring for the plants. Here, the gardener can water the plants on the wider, lower bench with no inconvenience. The top shelf is shallower, which allows more space for plants but has a higher and more difficult reach.

OPPOSITE: The interior of this lattice garden shed maintains a pleasing organization. Counter-height worktables, some with storage shelves underneath, sit on a gravel floor, with plenty of space between the work areas for moving around. The lath construction diffuses the light and permits good air circulation.

ABOVE: An English conservatory shows the jungle-like effect of massed exotic plants and vines. Conservatories became fashionable in England in the mid-nineteenth century. These large, light-filled glasshouses were built for growing tropical plants that needed warmth and sunshine all winter long. Conservatories, either free-standing or attached to a house, were often decorated with wicker or cast-iron furniture and used for socializing. These structures today provide all the light and space necessary for starting seeds indoors.

LEFT: Grape vines trained on wires across the top of this traditional glass and wood greenhouse offer both shade and ornament, as well as delicious fruit. Wide tables provide the gardener with enough space to experiment with lots of different plants.

ABOVE: Sunlight brightens this toolshed, which is filled with gardening supplies. Rakes, buckets, and containers stand on the floor while small tools and sundries fill the floor-to-ceiling shelves next to the window.

ABOVE: Pots of every size belong in the potting shed. These classic terra-cotta flowerpots have sloping sides and drainage holes in the bottom. Although clay containers are porous and dry out more quickly than their plastic counterparts, they tend to look better in the garden because their natural color and material blend well with the plants in and around them.

ABOVE: When a shed is compact in size, orderliness becomes crucial for its efficient use. Here, natural light enters the potting shed through a decorative roundel. The work surface is low and most easily accessible when the gardener is seated on a stool. Small tools hang on the walls, and beneath the table potting soil is stored in a brick bin, while deep drawers house seeds and other gardening supplies.

ABOVE: This utilitarian space beckons gardeners with its cheerful disarray. The conspicuous depth of the potting bench makes it particularly useful for accommodating projects and pots of all sizes. A cubby affixed to the wall provides storage for small items, while a bucket full of stakes and other garden implements stands at the ready. Whitewashed walls brighten a space that might appear gloomy if the original red brick had been left unpainted.

ABOVE: In autumn, the gardener assesses the bounty of the growing season. The roses and lavender of summer, now dried, delicate, and ready for use in winter crafts, join freshly picked apples and stacks of pots on the potting bench. Because apples keep ripening off the tree, it's important to store them at low temperatures to slow the process—a dark, unheated potting shed offers the perfect spot. The ripest fruit should be eaten immediately and not stored. Here, each apple is carefully wrapped and set in a box to protect it from bruising.

ABOVE: On sunny days, natural light from the doors and windows may be enough to illuminate a small potting shed, but on darker days or in the evenings it's useful to have electric lights. This shed has been wired for electricity (note the light switch near the door) to allow the gardener to work at any time of day and when the weather is rainy or overcast.

ABOVE: This potting table is clearly in active use. The gardener fills small pots with soil, sows the seeds, and labels the flats or the individual pots using indelible marker and wooden tags. The drop-leaf of the table can be easily raised when extra work surface is required, but when not needed stays neatly dropped to provide more room to move about.

OPPOSITE: This combination greenhouse and potting room has a large skylight that opens for good ventilation, which is crucial for growing plants indoors. Like most greenhouses, this one contains shelves for plants at different stages of growth and a potting bench with storage below. A basket on the wall recalls gathering the harvest, and a plain vine wreath brings floral crafts to mind.

LEFT: The potting bench in this solar greenhouse has plentiful light, storage, a sink, and a substantial work area. The solar collectors provide all the heat necessary to keep gardening activities going all winter.

OPPOSITE: Potting sheds can be as simple or as elegant as a gardener's taste and budget allows. Any enthusiast would delight in this shed's tiled mosaic floor, wooden walls, and excellent natural light, which gives the shed a warm and earthy glow. Beyond its relative luxury, the basics are also here—storage for containers, potting soil, and other gardening equipment, and a large sink for watering plants and cleaning pots and tools.

ABOVE: The weather outside is snowy, but inside this sunroom it's warm and bright enough for plants to thrive. In cold climates, a sunroom or greenhouse addition may provide not only indoor gardening space but also a pleasant, cozy place to relax.

ABOVE: Layered storage highlights the main work area in this custom sun space. The work center has a wide tabletop for holding containers for planting and vases for flower arranging. A sink deep enough to accommodate tall vases provides water for conditioning and arranging flowers and for soaking out the air bubbles in newly potted plants. On the middle level, plastic bins of compost and other soil amendments sit on a shelf, while at the base large plastic storage bins hold bagged seed starting mix and potting soil. The room's colors—green and a natural stained wood—reflect the landscape on the other side of the glass. Adjustable shades help control the amount of light in the room.

Chapter Four

SPACES FOR DRYING AND CONDITIONING FLOWERS AND HERBS

*G*ardeners like to share their bounty with friends. A bouquet of fresh flowers in a jar on a sick colleague's doorstep, stoppered containers filled with dried herbs for a cousin who loves to cook, and a grapevine wreath trimmed with dried wildflowers for a neighbor are some of the gifts that can come from the garden shed.

Sheds that are dry, airy, warm, and rather dark provide excellent conditions for drying herbs and flowers. Many thin-leaved herbs like rosemary, thyme, and oregano dry well when they are bunched in groups of about five sprigs, tied together, and hung by strings upside down from hooks, rafters, or a clothesline. Some flowers and foliage plants like artemisia, strawflower, hydrangea, goldenrod, and celosia also dry well in bunches. The inflorescences of many ornamental grasses dry beautifully and make elegant autumn bouquets that last for months.

Conditioning cut flowers can be a messy task best suited for potting areas with hot and cold water taps. This process swells the plant stems with water and makes them hard. Before soaking the stems in water, it's important to remove excess leaves and thorns, especially those that would be below the water line in the vase. Cut the stems cleanly on the diagonal and immerse them in a sterile bucket or jar of fresh water. For most flowers warm water is suitable for conditioning, but for woody stems hot water does a better job. Place the bucket in a cool, dark area, for several hours to overnight, until the stems are ready for arranging.

OPPOSITE: This combined summer kitchen and potting shed offers prime storage for canned, homemade vegetables and beans. Cookbooks sit on a bottom shelf near the sink, accessible but comfortably out of the way of dirt and water. Bunches of herbs hang from the rafters, while cut flowers in a tall pail soak up water in the deep sink.

RIGHT: Flower-filled window boxes and lush borders outside the garden shed allow a minimum of steps from the flower source to the work table.

ABOVE: This barn, with its warm, dark, dry space and excellent ventilation, makes an excellent location for drying flowers and storing them. Although darkness is not a necessity, it helps brightly colored flowers maintain their color throughout the drying and storing process.

OPPOSITE: This deep potting bench holds a jumble of containers and flowering plants. A strawberry jar stands as the first task of the day, ready to be filled with colorful flowers. Empty clay pots and garden shoes sit on a shelf below the work surface, while a garbage can contains plant material intended for the compost pile.

RIGHT: Baskets of dried flowers cover a table, ready to be added to lovely arrangements. Above the bench handmade baskets hang on hooks, while long gardening tools line the walls nearby.

OPPOSITE: A feeling of repose pervades the interior of this rustic garden shed. Accessories sometimes reserved for the house, such as a cheerful rug and a profusion of wicker baskets, create an aura of warmth and comfort. More than a place to dry herbs and blooms it's a retreat where the gardener can mull the discoveries of the day, store hats and smocks, and craft with flowers and herbs fresh from the garden.

LEFT: The flamboyant postmodern design of this cutting room cannot obscure the basic practicality of the space. The tiled floor and counter are easy to clean, and copious shelves for vases and containers line the walls. Daylight enters the room from a glass-block skylight. A sink provides hot and cold water for conditioning different kinds of flowers—room temperature for the tender blooms of spring, warm water for most flowers and foliage, and hot water for the woody stems of flowering shrubs and trees. A trompe l'oeil painting provides a vista from the window above the sink. In this sunny garden scene, it's always summer, no matter what the season is outdoors.

OPPOSITE: For flower arrangers, the garden shed is the ideal stop between the yard and the house. At the potting bench, gardeners can trim and condition their stems of flowers and foliage before arranging them in vases. The trip to the garden shed helps keep the house free from excess water and plant material, since only the final arrangement will come indoors.

PHOTO CREDITS